THE FAST FORWARD WINNER

(Revised Version)

by Bob Rathbun

Zhana Publishing © 2018
publishing@zhanacorporation.com

ISBN: 978-0-9987855-0-9

Table of Contents

Introduction

The Fast Forward Winner^{TM} program empowers people to realize their dreams by visualizing them and then taking the steps necessary to achieve those dreams. I believe strongly that everyone has been put on this Earth for a reason, and I want to help people discover what they are meant to do with their lives.

Anyone can achieve his/her dreams. I know because I did, and I am no different than anyone else. My dream of being a sportscaster had humble beginnings in my childhood. I grew up in a lower middle class mobile home community in North Carolina and I loved sports, especially listening to the broadcasts on the radio.

So one Sunday afternoon when I was 12-years-old, I called one of our two local radio stations — WSTP, and told the announcer (John Bolcer) how much I loved the radio station and especially the sports broadcasts. Then something remarkable happened. Instead of just thanking me like he could have done, he invited me to come down for a tour of the radio station. I loved it and became a regular there on Sundays. I did chores like taking out the trash, filing, etc. And then one afternoon the sportscaster dropped in and John introduced us. Again, something remarkable happened. Instead of just shaking my hand, this sportscaster offered to let me help with the American Legion baseball games.

So you could find me at Newman Ballpark helping out by doing things like keeping score and getting Cokes. Then one day, out of the blue, the sportscaster tells me that it's time for me to make my debut, and he's going to let me broadcast the bottom of the 7th inning. I don't remember exactly what I said, but I do remember that a player named Joey Brown hit one out of the park that day. When the sportscaster got the mic back, he said that he'd been waiting all season to call a home run and that naturally it had happened when a 12-year-old kid was announcing. That sportscaster was Marty Brennaman, and he is now a Hall of Fame broadcaster for the

Cincinnati Reds.

When you act on your dreams, people are put in your path that you would never imagine. I got to know Warner Fusselle, who was the WSTP news guy at the time. I also had the privilege of knowing Joe Ferebee, who is the man who coached the American Legion team and is the winningest amateur baseball coach in North Carolina history.

As a teenager, besides knowing everyone at the radio station, I got the chance to meet some other key people because the National Sportscaster sand Sportswriters Association is headquartered in Salisbury, North Carolina, and they always hold an annual awards ceremony. So when I was old enough to drive, the NSSA transportation committee had me ferry all the big name announcers from the Charlotte airport to Salisbury for this big annual event. On the 45 minute drive from the airport, I got the chance to talk with all these guys and eventually got to work on the committee as a host.

More breaks came my way when a Wyoming sportscaster Leo Morris fell in love with Salisbury, moved there, and asked me to help with the college football and basketball broadcasts for Wake Forest. Leo started coming to the NSSA Awards ceremony as a state winner and eventually moved his family to North Carolina. His son, Ron, an aspiring sportswriter, helped me land a job writing sports for the local daily newspaper, *The Salisbury Post*, and I did that for several years. This experience let me see the newspaper side of the sports world and gave me a fantastic journalism background, all before I left high school.

During college, I attended UNC-Charlotte and worked in sports information, a job which allowed me to be exposed to yet another side of the business. Then my old radio station contacted me to ask me to come back, offering me a full-time job announcing sports. So I transferred back to work and attended Catawba College full-time.

From these affirming experiences, I learned that if you just honor that feeling of something you would like to do, there is no telling where you will go and what you will achieve. I know because it happened to me. Everything starts with a thought. The Fast Forward Winner[TM] program is designed to take that thought and put it into motion.

I remember affirming that "I'm going to be a major league announcer." I was able to visualize my dream and then go back and take all the steps necessary to get to where I am today. Now I'm doing what I love, and loving what I do. That's what the Fast Forward Winner[TM] program is all about. When we recognize our dream and act upon it, something magical happens to our lives and to the lives of the people we touch.

The Fast Forward

Most books have a *foreword*. This one has a *forward* – a *fast forward*. In this manual I'm going to share with you what has happened to me in life and how I got where I am today. And I hope that in sharing with you, I can save you the trouble of making the same mistakes I made. I also hope you will see that you can achieve whatever you want because it happened for me, and you are no different from me, so it can happen for you too.

This manual will allow you to take your idea and fast forward into the future so you can see yourself doing whatever you dream. By "fast forward" I mean that you will be able to project ahead to the end result and then come back to work with this manual to complete the practical steps necessary to make your dream a winning reality for you. Just because I use the word "fast" doesn't mean what you want can be achieved quickly or without work. There are no shortcuts.

To get started, I want you to think about something you have wanted to do for a long time but for some reason you never did. The following are a few of the most common excuses people have for not pursuing their dreams:

1. I've dreamed about doing something but never thought I could (fear of failure, financial obstacles, lack of ability, etc.)

Fear of failure might be one of the most common obstacles people face in starting a new project. You dream big dreams but can't seem to turn the ignition switch on. Well, welcome to the club. Even the most successful among us have had those fears. In the sports arena, one of the greatest athletes of all time is basketball superstar Michael Jordan. But early on, he had a coach tell him he didn't have the ability to make the freshman high school team when he tried out. Now, with an unprecedented six championship rings, Air Jordan is living proof that the only person responsible for your success or failure is you and that you will never know what you can accomplish until you try.

"I've missed more than 9,000 shots in my career. I've lost almost 300 games. Twenty- six times I've been trusted to take the game winning shot and missed. I've failed over and over and over again in my life. And that is why I succeed." – Michael Jordan

He never let failure stop him from trying or keep him from trying again. Nor should fear of failure prevent you from getting started.

2. I've always wanted to pursue my dream but life keeps getting in the way. (I got married, had kids, and now I have a mortgage and am too old to get started.)

Harland Sanders created Kentucky Fried Chicken, the "Finger Lickin' Good" meal which became a fast-food sensation in the 1960s. Sanders was already 40-years-old when he began cooking chicken for customers at his service station in Corbin, Kentucky.

According to his corporate biography, "Over the next nine years, he perfected his secret blend of 11 herbs and spices and the basic cooking technique that is still used today." Sanders became well-known in his home state, but it took another 20 years before he began franchising Kentucky Fried Chicken restaurants around the country. By 1964, when he sold his stake in the company, the Colonel's chicken was being sold in the company's popular paper buckets at over 600 outlets nationwide. Sanders continued to appear as the company's spokesman for more than a decade: with his white suit, string tie and cane, he had the look of a courtly Southern gentleman. - www.answers.com

So as you can see, you are never too old to get started.

3. I'm inspired by the stories of people who see a wrong and try to right it. There may be a social issue at your high school or workplace that prompts you to take action. And if there is no organization to join, start one!

In 1980 Candy Lightner founded Mothers Against Drunk Driving (MADD). This powerful group was created because of a personal tragedy when her twelve-year-old daughter, Cari, was killed by a drunk driver.

Candy Lightner transformed a tragedy into a remarkable effort to educate, inform, and change society. She headed MADD for eight years.

Today MADD's effect is felt worldwide with chapters in all fifty states and many international affiliates. Its goals are to educate, prevent, and punish people who choose to drive while intoxicated. This organization has become powerful enough to cause judicial reforms throughout the United States.

Lightner's outreach has made an impact through her lectures, speeches, writings, and personal appearances. She speaks about survivors of alcohol-related crashes, victim's rights, legislative advocacy, grass roots organizations, and the need to recognize the contributions of women and children in our society.

Lightner is often featured on radio and television, including the Lifetime Television Network, *Good Morning America*, and many other programs. She also appears before Congress to appeal for stricter drunk driving laws. In addition, she speaks to organizations and businesses as a consultant.

Her books include, *Guilty Until Proven Innocent* and *Who's Responsible or How to Have a Party*. Her articles have appeared in national magazines, newspapers, and legal journals. Lightner has been awarded many honors, including honorary degrees in public service from Kutztown University in Kutztown, Pennsylvania and Marymount College in Johnstown, Pennsylvania.

4. I have tried pursuing my dream, but I keep getting knocked off track. (Passed over for promotions, took a dead-end job, got laid off, etc.)

Mary Kay Ash was born on May 12, 1918 in Hot Wells, Texas. When she was six years old, she had to look after her ill grandfather while her mother was working to provide for the family. Throughout her life, Mary Kay's mother had a huge impact on her daughter, and she attributed her indomitable spirit to her mother who encouraged her with the words, "You can do it."

While she was studying to become a doctor, she started selling products for Stanley Home part-time. She proved so adept at selling that she soon began working full-time and went on to work at World Gift where she eventually became a Sales Director. But when Kay was passed over for a promotion time after time, she decided to call it quits after 25 years of corporate sales.

Mary Kay then turned her attention to writing a book which turned out to be the plan for her business. On September 13, 1963, with $5,000 in savings, she opened her dream cosmetics business. After buying the formula for a skin-care cream, Kay started operating from a small Dallas storefront. With nine salespeople, or beauty consultants as she called her team, they made nearly $200,000 profit in the first year of operation.

The company's success soared, and to this day, it remains one of the largest private firms in the United States. Mary Kay Inc. also rates well in regularly performed surveys of "Best Company to Work For". © Financial-Inspiration.com

So as you can see from the examples of Michael Jordan, Harland Sanders, Candy Lightner and Mary Kay, there are no excuses for not succeeding in achieving your dream.

First you have to identify exactly what your **seed dream** is (Chapter 1). Then you will have to determine the steps necessary to put your **dream** into **action** (Chapter 2). After that, you will learn how to dig for **pay dirt** and do the work it will take to succeed (Chapter 3). Next you will discover how to develop **expert confidence** in what you are doing (Chapter 4). Then you will take some **time out** to evaluate your progress (Chapter 5). Last, you will learn how to hit the **curve balls** that life throws you so you can overcome the problems which will inevitably arise in the pursuit of your dream (Chapter 6).

I don't know where you are in your journey on the way to fulfilling your life's purpose. But I do know that by picking up this manual, you have taken an important first step. So let's not waste any more time. Turn the page and let's get started making your dreams become a reality.

The beginning is the most important part of any work.
- *Plato*

Successful People Are Dreamers

*Excerpt from **The Daily Guru**©*

Your dreams are your vision of where you'll be after the battle; your prize at the end of your journey to success.

Your goals are the steps you take to finally attain your prize.

Unless you're willing to work hard and establish some discipline in your life, all of your dreams will be pipe dreams, little mental fantasy trips that will never materialize.

Make concrete steps toward fulfilling your ultimate dream, and start with solid objectives and goals.

Your dreams are where you want to go; your goals are how you get there. The indispensable first step to getting the things you want out of life is this:

- Decide what you want.
- Don't be afraid to think big and dare to be great.
- Dreamers are not content with mediocrity. They never dream of going halfway.
- People with goals succeed because they know where they're going.

Chapter 1

Seed Dream

"You'll see it when you believe it."
- Dr. Wayne Dyer

Seed Dream

What Is A Seed Dream?

A Seed Dream is a goal or a vision that you have for yourself which can go back as far as your childhood. It is something you can really see yourself doing even though it may be seemingly out of reach to you right now.

The greatest example I can use to illustrate this is my own personal story. I believe that a seed dream was planted in me to become a sports broadcaster. It was all I really wanted to do since I was 12-years-old. In fact, it was all I could think about, and everything I was involved in revolved around this dream. So I took action on that dream and have been broadcasting ever since. I'll talk in more detail about this later in this manual, but for right now, I want you to think of something that gets you excited. This should be something that warms your heart, but also something you are willing to work hard to achieve.

To identify your seed dream, think of something that you can get enthusiastic about. It's an interesting word, enthusiasm. Its root is "enthu" which translated from the early Greeks, means "from God." If there is an idea that has you feeling enthusiastic, then you are probably on to something related to your personal seed dream. Your enthusiasm is a good indicator that there is divinity in your idea that makes it right for you.

Why Are Seed Dreams Important?

We were, I believe, placed on the Earth for a purpose bigger than we are; a Divine Purpose. Perhaps our greatest challenge in life is to have the necessary courage to recognize this purpose and act on it. Learning how to recognize and then execute your seed dream will come in the following chapters.

Now is the time for you to make a positive impact on the world. There are plenty of negative influences out there. If you don't believe me, pick up today's newspaper or turn on the TV or radio news. What you want to do with your Seed Dream is to start the turnaround by taking something that you care about and turning it into something tangible and positive.

The fact that you've invested your time in this manual tells me that you, like me, are searching for some real meaning in your life. I do believe that when we choose a path such as this, we are engaging in a process that will make the world a better place.

The first step is doing something that makes you happy because then you are contributing to the overall positive energy of the planet. And that is a good place to start improving conditions for yourself and those around you.

As you develop your Seed Dream, it's essential to eliminate doubt right away. It's important to have clean, pure, unadulterated enthusiasm for what you are doing. If you have any doubts, it may be because you are thinking about what others will say about your dream. How the world views what you are doing is not important.

Let's make a pact now that what you are doing here is meaningful work, and you should not ultimately care about how others judge your actions.

Another way to know that your dream is important is to give it the energy test. If your idea is worthy of time and effort, you will be granted creative ideas, personal power, new relationships, and unbelievable experiences to help you succeed. Seed dreams give us a hidden energy and determination we did not know we had. They also activate helpers in the Universe (Angels, if you prefer) to arrange the right people, places, and events in the exact order you need them so you can achieve your dream. But the dream can't become a reality until you take action. None of this universal power or energy will be yours until you take the steps necessary to put it in motion.

What are the Steps for Acheiving Seed Dreams?

1. The first order of business is to brainstorm the things that interest you or that you really have a desire to accomplish in your life. This process will mirror a goals-setting workshop (if you have ever done one of those), but our exercise takes a different tack. This one is going to put a smile on your face. This thing that you choose will give you an instant sense of well-being. Unlike a goal, which should be measurable and with a timeline to prod you, this seed dream will feel like something you could do with little effort. It will not take little effort, I can assure you, but it will feel that way. That is your first clue that you are on your personal 'right track'. Whether it is big or little in the eyes of the world

doesn't matter. There is no need to share your dream with anyone. In fact, I will ask you here at the outset to keep what you are thinking about to yourself until you are ready to take it 'out on the street.' Keep it personal right now, so you don't lose your momentum by any possible negative feedback you might receive from others.

2. Determine which pursuits really resonate with you – maybe some even go back to things you have wanted to do since childhood. When I was 12, I had absolutely no doubt that picking up a telephone and calling a radio station was the right thing for me to do. I believe this was because the idea of radio and broadcasting was something that resonated with me. And I had no idea what resonate even meant when I was 12! But looking back now, I can truly say that my break into the business came when I acted on ideas when I had 'no doubt.' If you allow doubt to creep into your thoughts—even at this early point — you have a problem. If you are having doubts right now about doing something — stop!! Where are your doubts coming from? Is yours just a weak idea of something you want to do, or is it resonating with you as something you are enthusiastic about doing? I want you to feel good about your choice in this initial phase of the Fast Forward WinnerTM program.

3. If you are not sure just what this Seed Dream should look, feel, taste, or smell like, look for a recurring theme. You might want to jot down some ideas. Let yourself go. Don't stop writing. Just fill the page with thoughts and ideas. Write them out in shorthand. You won't need complete sentences. These notes will

be the starting point for determining your Seed Dream and where your greatness lies.

4. On the next page I am going to ask you to begin a very serious exercise. If you need to, turn off the TV or the mobile device and really listen to your heart. What is your soul trying to say to you? As Dr. Robert Schuller asks, "what could you accomplish if you knew you could not fail?"

Life is one indivisible whole. The games we played in childhood can give us clues as to our deepest wants and desires. For myself, I can remember playing a game called Strat- O-Matic Baseball. It was a table game played with dice and player cards for virtually every player in the big leagues. The outcomes were skewed toward the players' actual results in games played from the previous season. And as I played these games (the Red Sox were my team), I would broadcast the play-by-play of the action. So even as a child, I was acting out my dream with the games I played. Think back to your childhood. What games did you play? Can you think of any which reflect your deepest desires? What did you want to be when you grew up? Your memories can be the signals which will give you clues about what you are truly interested in and passionate about. I discovered my Seed Dream at age 12. You can do the same thing, no matter how old you are right now. But you do have to want to act on that desire.

Seed Dream Exercise #1

Because life is one indivisible whole, the circle of our dreams never ends. Around the outside of the circle below, write down some things you are passionate about doing. These could include things like: learning a foreign language, tutoring kids, reading to the elderly, volunteering at a hospital, and being self-employed, just to name a few.

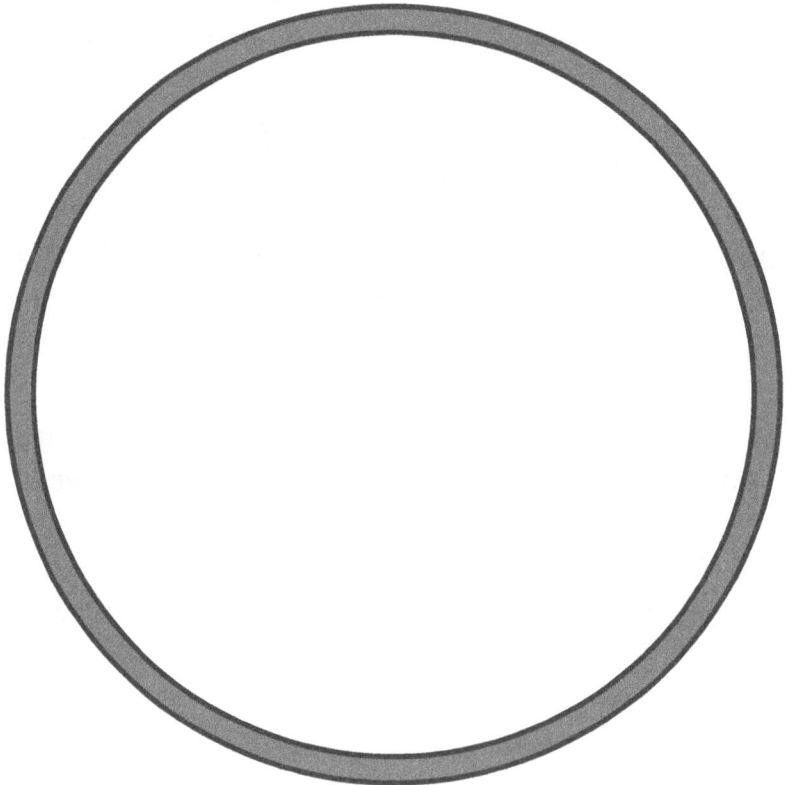

Take a look at the things you have written around the circle and see if you can find some recurring themes. Put those things in the middle of the circle.

Try to narrow down the theme(s) you have placed in the middle of the circle into something you really want to do (your Seed Dream). Write down what your seed dream is. Make sure that it is a true desire, and not something that nags at you and says to you, "yeah, that would be nice." I want this Seed Dream to be something that resonates deep within you and gets you excited thinking about the final outcome.

_____

_____

_____

_____

_____

_____

_____

_____

_____

_____

_____

_____

_____

_____

_____

_____

"The discipline of writing something down is the first step toward making it happen."

Lee Iacocca, former Chairman, Chrysler Corporation

Chapter 2

Dream Action

"Whatever you think you can do or believe you can do, begin it. Action has magic, grace and power in it."
- Johann Wolfgang von Goethe

Dream Action

What Is Dream Action?

Dream action is taking the action necessary to move closer to your dream. Dream Action requires having enough courage to make that leap of faith by trying something new or doing something differently. You have to be willing to take the first step – whatever that might be – and do something you have never done before.

Now you are going to need a little courage here! Don't let that doubt creep in! You've got your new idea but the action plan is still in its embryonic stage. The next item for you to plan is how you will set your dream in motion. By doing so, you will do two things: one, you will let the universe know that you are serious about this, so it can start aligning the people, places, and things you need to make it happen; and two, by taking those first steps, you will begin to gather valuable feedback. Take good notes along the way. You will refer to them in subsequent chapters.

Why is Dream Action important?

Generally speaking, your dreams and desires don't just fall into your lap. If you want to do something big or small, you have to take action. You have to step out of your comfort zone to create change.

Taking action gives your dream a purpose. A dream without action is just a dream. By taking the first step toward what it is you desire, you unleash great powers that were once dormant. When your dream reflects your positive, core beliefs and you choose to take action, you will find that you are the one "getting the breaks." Only when you are proactively pursuing your goals will the people, events, circumstances, and coincidences all begin to go your way, leading you closer and closer to the completion of your dream.

What are the Steps for taking Your Dream Action?

1. Make the decision to take action. As odd as this may sound, just making up your mind to take action and following through may be the most challenging aspect of this entire program for you. Don't become a victim of "paralysis by analysis!" As the folks at Nike^{TM} implore us in their ads, 'Just Do It.' Here's a secret: if you take that first step, the universe will take *its* first step. Your action is small compared to the immeasurable action the universe puts into place when you move forward with your dream. Now, is there any reason not to get started?

2. Don't worry whether the timing is right or how your dream will be received.

Early in my radio days, I sold commercials. I could have been a great salesman, but I was consumed by the fear of rejection. Oh, if I had known then what I know now! But here's what I want to share with you: I had a hard time back then making calls. I didn't understand the psychology of selling, or how to go about it. That fear stopped me from taking action! On our quest here, you have already chosen something which you are thrilled about, not something you are forced into like I was with selling commercials. The time is right for you and your plan — right now! Go for it!

3. If you still need more inspiration, read articles about how people with similar goals/dreams got started. There are many places to find such stories. John Maxwell offers a daily e-mail Leadership Wired which you can receive free via e- mail. The key is to make it a study. Reading this material should be a part of your daily routine like bathing and brushing your teeth.

Walt Disney never gave up on his dream even after he lost his first big-time character, Oswald the Lucky Rabbit. Studio owner Charles Mintz took both the character and animation team away from Disney when he tried to negotiate a higher fee. Down, but not out, Disney came up with the idea of Mortimer Mouse, later changing the name when his wife Lilly said, "How about Mickey?"

Let's consider a guy who never graduated from college. His first marriage ended in a bitter divorce, and he lost most of his savings in the stock market crash. Every business venture he tried, failed. But he kept asking questions: "What makes successful people successful? What are their methods?" He wanted to find the key to success, and he put his findings in a book. If you haven't read How to Win Friends and Influence People by Dale Carnegie, you should add that to your reading list.

4. Listen to positive motivational tapes from the masters. Fill your brain with upbeat messages and examples — get rid of that stinkin' thinkin' as motivational speaker Zig Ziglar would often say. Always keep learning and make it a part of who

you are. I always thought I was a pretty positive person. But it wasn't until I was exposed to motivational tapes and books that I realized my thinking was often out of line with my goals and dreams.

The maddening pace of the outside world always seems to accentuate the negative. We don't need that now or ever. By continually feeding your mind the good stuff, you will program yourself for success. Whatever you think about expands no matter whether your thoughts are positive or negative. Keep positive thoughts and ideas foremost in your consciousness. You can reinforce this daily by listening to the masters in this genre. I do. It works.

5. In sports, I have never met an elite athlete who didn't begin with the end in mind; he or she always has viewed themselves as a big time player and a winner. I want you to start from that same perspective. It's what the Fast Forward WinnerTM program is all about: start with an idea, Fast Forward to the end to see you doing it, being it, and then put a plan together to make it happen.

6. The act of getting started tells the Divine Power that you are serious about what you want and helps you begin organizing your universe in a way that will support you in your dream quest. Let's get back to Salisbury, North Carolina for a moment and when I was 12. I am convinced now that John Bolcer was placed in that spot as an announcer at WSTP *specifically* to take my phone call and invite me down to the station to launch my career. You could never convince me otherwise. It happened

because I was in right-alignment with my Seed Dream. It happened for me when I was 12, and it can happen for you right here, right now. That person is in place waiting for you. I am convinced of it. Make the call. Write the letter. Do it now!

Dream Action Exercise #1

Write two affirmation lines. The first one starts with "I am..." and explains who you want to be. For me, it was "I am a major league broadcaster." The second affirmation line begins "I will..." and states what action you will take in order to move closer to your dream.

I am

_____

_____

_____

_____

_____

I will

_____

_____

_____

_____

_____

You should keep your dream private initially, especially from people who would give you negative feedback by telling you all the reasons you can't do what you want. There's power behind any goal that you set that tends to dissipate if you share it too early in the game. When you reach out to make this thing happen, other people will have to be involved, but just make sure that the people you choose to share your dream with will be supportive.

Often people want to wait for the perfect time to do something. It's easy to make excuses and to procrastinate.

You say to yourself that right before the holidays isn't a good time to start anything new or that you are just too busy at work or school and when things slow down you will have some time to get started. There are always a million reasons for not doing something. Trust me; the timing is never going to be perfect. You're just going to have to take that leap of faith right now and – just do it.

Dream Action Exercise #2

In order to help you see your ultimate goal, you have to clearly visualize what you want. In this exercise, imagine what it will be like to achieve your dream. Think about all the sights, sounds, surroundings, etc. that will accompany the successful completion of your goal. If you have never been exposed to the environment/surroundings (in my case that would have been a radio station or a major league stadium/arena) then take a field trip to the place or research it on the internet or look through pictures in books or magazines. This action will help make your visualization more real. The better you can visualize your dream, the more likely you are to achieve it. Use the lines below to describe your visualization in details and/or use the blank space to draw what you envision.

_____
_____
_____
_____
_____
_____
_____
_____
_____
_____
_____
_____
_____
_____
_____

"The more that you read, the more things you will know.
The more that you learn, the more places you'll go."
- Dr. Seuss

Chapter 3

Digging for Pay Dirt

"You are the same today as you will be in five years except for two things: the people you meet and the books you read."
Charlie "Tremendous" Jones

Digging for Pay Dirt

What Is Digging For Pay Dirt?

"**P**ay dirt" is a nickname for gravel with a high concentration of gold and other precious metals in it. Often times when I broadcast football games, I will use the phrase, "digging for pay dirt" to describe the ball carrier making a really hard run toward the end zone. This is when the player is really driving his cleats into the turf, getting good traction, and building great speed and momentum in order to reach the end zone and score.

"Digging for pay dirt" is an indication of the work it takes to get to your ultimate goal. For you, these will be the steps you need to take to put your dream in motion. Now is the time for you to move your dream out of the thought stage and take action to do the work to make it a reality. Up to this point, you have just been thinking about what you want to do. Now you are putting a plan together to make it happen.

Why Is Digging For Pay Dirt Important?

Digging for pay dirt is important because it is the crucial first step toward the realization of your goals. In order to bring your dreams to life, you must start digging for more information about what you want to do and what it takes to achieve success. Learning more about your topic should increase your excitement and enthusiasm for your project and take your interest to a new level.

As you move from dreaming to doing, you will build momentum through taking action. The more you dig and become immersed in your stated goal, the more you will learn that one discovery leads to another. You get more and more excited as you gain knowledge and begin to acquire expertise in your endeavor. Inevitably someone will stop you and say, "Boy, you are really excited and passionate about this!" The pleasure of getting that kind of reinforcement will naturally amp up your excitement level.

One of the additional benefits of this research and development is that you will be viewed as a leader. You will be recognized as someone who is a goal-oriented person who takes charge and is driven to create a positive outcome.

Think of your own circle of friends and people who have embodied the reputation of really knowing their stuff. You may know someone who is a good cook, and every time you think of that person, you say to yourself, "she can whip up anything." Or maybe you know someone who is an outstanding volunteer. This is the person that other people always ask for help when they want to make their project or endeavor a success. These types of people will stand out in your mind as the people who know what they are talking about and always get the job done. Receiving this kind of recognition is one of the many benefits of going that extra mile to become an expert in your field.

What Are The Steps In Digging For Pay Dirt?

1. As you research, you should realize that there are a lot of options to choose from in your field of interest. As you go into more depth, you will discover which areas most suit you, and then you can get more specific and narrow your focus.
2. Talk to people! I talk to coaches and players all the time. And if you keep probing, they will tell you

things you didn't know, sharing stories and connections that will not only provide valuable information, but may very well put you in touch with a key contact that you did not know existed.

3. Make a timeline of when events happen. Connect the dots. You can learn a great deal about trends, timing, and the key players in your field.

4. As you are doing your research and reading books on your topic, make a note of "ah-ha" moments. I am asking you to not simply *read*, but to devour these books, with key thoughts, sentences, and paragraphs underlined and highlighted. Then you will have them available to refer back to when you need those insights to inspire you, or you are looking for the right piece of information for the next step in your process.

5. Learn the ancillary stories. There are the major players and then there are the minor players. Get to know why the minor players are as important as the major players.

6. Learn the specialized terminology for your area, so you will be able to speak the language to others in your field.

In any endeavor, there is a history. Research it. Think to yourself: "Here's what these guys did and here are the results they got. Here's what this group did, and here are the results they got." Write down what you think is important and want to remember for future reference.

Digging For Pay Dirt Exercise #1

Research and then write down any history you know about your endeavor

_____

_____

_____

_____

_____

_____

_____

_____

_____

_____

_____

_____

_____

_____

In the following chart, write down the action that various groups or individuals took, along with the results they achieved.

Action	Result

One good way to organize the information you collect is to plot key points on a line. After you research the main events, you will find that some things will overlap and intertwine.

When researching a topic, I like to put together a timeline of events so that I can tie the subject material to other events that may lead me down other paths to new information or linkage back to the primary subject. For example, if I were researching Hall of Fame football coach Bill Parcells, I would start at the beginning of Bill's high school and college career and put something down on paper like this:

Name	Played at	Coached by	Coached at	When	Under/With
Bill Parcells	River Dell High			'79	
	Colgate	Frank Foldberg	Hastings	'63	
			Wichita State	'65	George Karras
			Army	'66-69	Tom Cahill
			FSU	'70-72	Bill Peterson
			Vanderbilt	'73-74	Steve Sloan
			Texas Tech	'75-77	Steve Sloan
			NY Giants	'79	Ray Perkins
			NE Patriots	'80	Ron Erhardt

Thanks to Dr. Paul G. Schempp
www.PerformanceMattersInc.com

After compiling my timeline, I would do my on-line research to begin connecting the dots. Here's a story I came across:

*Six degrees of **Bill Parcells** -- Coach has many ties to the game* by JAIME ARON, THE ASSOCIATED PRESS Date: 02-01-2004

HOUSTON - Skip the Bud Bowl, Lingerie Bowl, and other Super Bowl spin-offs. The best secondary entertainment leading up to Sunday's big game is playing Six Degrees of **Bill Parcells**.

(Here's a nugget buried in the story. Note the graph above that shows Bill as an assistant at FSU. This story links all of the coaches that Parcells has worked with over the years that were coaching during Super Bowl XXXVIII. That game, in Houston, Texas, saw New England defeat the Carolina Panthers.)

On the Carolina side, the strongest link with Bill is offensive coordinator Dan Henning, whom **Parcells** has said is "one guy, if I call on him and I need something, I kind of feel like he'd be there for me."

Their friendship began in 1970, when they were assistant coaches at Florida State. They were in New England at the same time in the '90s, with Henning coaching Boston College and **Parcells** running the Patriots. A few years later, Henning was on **Parcells'** staff on the Jets. - *Copyright 2004 Bergen Record Corp. All rights reserved.*

Story by story, bit by bit, you start to put pieces together about your subject. If it's sports, you can learn where people were and when, how the team prevailed that season, as well as who the players and other coaches were. You have to have a little Sherlock Holmes in you! Do a little digging, a little investigating. The payoff will come in due time.

In January of 2007, Parcells retired from coaching. When he left his last job as the head coach of the Dallas Cowboys, all of the reports talked about what he had accomplished, and many stories paid tribute to the legacy that he was leaving behind. Chicago Bears coach Lovie Smith said, "We're losing one of our all-time great coaches in our profession."

After learning from his mentors, Parcells returned that knowledge and wisdom to his protégés in his years as a head coach. His influence will remain because of all the coaches who worked for him, from three-time Super Bowl champion, Bill Belichick of New England, to New Orleans' Sean Payton, the 2007 NFL coach of the year.

Tom Coughlin of the Giants and Romeo Crennel of Cleveland also paid their dues under Parcells. "Bill's an excellent football coach and a very good friend," Coughlin told the AP. "We're going to miss Bill Parcells on the sideline, and we'll miss him in the NFC East."

Parcells' greatest trait as a coach was his ability to turn around downtrodden clubs. All four teams he coached had losing records before he arrived, but all four were in the playoffs by his second season. No other coach has taken that many franchises to the postseason. What he did as a coach was truly remarkable.

Dream Action Exercise #2

Make a timeline of when events happen and then compare them with each other. You can add your own column headings.

Your Timeline:

Once you have this information, you are ready to interview experts in that area/field.

High school and college students often ask how to get into broadcasting. What they're really asking is: "How can I be a broadcaster like you?" What I tell them is this: Being the play-by-play announcer at a sporting event is very exciting, but it might not be for you. What I want you to do is sample a little bit of everything that is in the broadcasting field to see what resonates with you. See what feels like the best fit for you. It might be producing, writing, operating a camera, or being a videotape operator. But you won't know that until you try a little bit of everything first. Not everybody is going to know at age 12 what they are going to do with the rest of their lives like I did. My business is a very exciting profession, and there are many ways to be a part of it – not just as a play-by-play announcer.

You can't do everything by yourself. I encourage youngsters to talk to experts to gain insight and wisdom. Mentors can help you but only if you ask them. Most people will be more than willing to help you.

As you prepare to talk to people, have your list of questions ready. After you ask your initial question, listen carefully and follow-up with a second question. You should never have the second question scripted. The absence of a scripted second question will force you to ask another question based on the answer you have just received. This makes it mandatory that you listen to what is being said!

The format would be:
Q1 (prepared question)
A1 (their answer)
Q2 (ad lib question based on their answer 1)
A2 (their follow-up answer)

I often have to interview players and coaches in my job. When deciding what to ask first, I always make it a point to tell my guest what is coming. I might say to the athlete, "Hey, this is going to be easy. Just a couple of questions, and I'll start with that home run in the bottom of the 8th." This does two things. First, it puts the guest at ease, so he or she can already start thinking about an answer. Second, it lets that person know that this is not going to be like *60 Minutes* or the Spanish Inquisition.

The interview begins.

"*I'm speaking with Joe Jones of the Bad News Bears. Joe, that homer you hit in the bottom of the 8th decided the game. Tell us about it!*" Question 1.

"*Yeah, it felt good. The pitcher kinda surprised me, but I got it all and hit it out.*"

Answer 1

"*You say he surprised you? What do you mean by that?*" Question 2.

"*Well, I thought he would try to blow me away with the fast ball, but I figured I might see a curve, since he struck me out on that pitch earlier. So I guessed right with the breaking ball.*" Answer 2.

Dream Action Exercise #3

Use the following prepared questions as a starting point for interviewing people. As you gain more information and experience, you can come up with some questions of your own. Write the answers you get on the lines below the question. It's also good to listen carefully to the answer to the question and follow up with another question. You might consider recording the interview and transcribing the answers later.

1. "How did you get started?"

_____

_____

_____

_____

_____

_____

2. "What do I need to study/learn?"

_____

_____

_____

_____

_____

_____

3. "Who were your mentors?"

_____

_____

_____

_____
_____

4. "What is the most important lesson you learned?"

_____
_____
_____
_____
_____
_____

5. "What do you think I need to know to get started?"

_____
_____
_____
_____
_____
_____

6. "Who else should I talk to?"

_____
_____
_____
_____
_____
_____

7. Create your own questions to ask based on your research.

_____
_____

_____

_____

_____

_____

_____

_____

_____

_____

_____

_____

_____

_____

You can learn more information from people by getting them to talk about themselves. After you talk with several people, put their timelines together. You can say something like, "Oh, Fred, I see you were here the same year that Mary moved here." When you show you've done some homework and research, you are viewed in a more professional light and have set yourself apart from others.

Chapter 4

Expert Confidence

"Let what you say be the tip of the iceberg to all you know."
- Jim Rohn

Expert Confidence

What Is Expert Confidence?

Let's say you are contemplating taking a self-defense course. You are concerned that you might not know what to do if placed in a compromised position. You investigate the classes available and make your selection. On the first day, your teacher shows up and says to you, "Mr. Rathbun, how would you like to walk down any city street unafraid?" My response would be, "Let's get started." That feeling is the same feeling I want you to have when it comes to the knowledge of your subject material. I call it, Expert Confidence.

When you are an expert in your particular area, you will have unshakable confidence in your ability to communicate all aspects of what you know. I view each broadcast that I make or speech that I give like a final exam in school. That is the level of preparation I asked of you in Chapter 3. Now it is time to expand upon the knowledge base you have acquired.

It is very important to me in my business of public speaking to know what I am talking about. There is a public trust placed in me when it comes to speaking. I view that trust as sacred. If I violate it, I am letting down my audience. I can't do that. Do I make mistakes? Of course I do. Do I get things wrong sometimes? Absolutely. But these mistakes are things I could have avoided if I had prepared better.

Why Is Expert Confidence Important?

There are two schools of thought that I want you to consider in the area of expert confidence. First, if your idea is something that you ultimately plan to take to the marketplace, it will be important for you to have it well researched. If your time and money will be on the line, give yourself every chance to succeed by knowing your subject from top to bottom.

Even though a person is never a complete and total expert on anything, you need to learn as much as you can about your subject. That way, if you are asked, you could talk for hours about every nuance. Second, have something good to say. There are two ways to have the tallest building in town. You can tear everyone else's down, or you can build yours higher. Be a builder.

Criticizing and second guessing is the easy way out. Again, in the marketplace, you will be called on to 'sell' your new idea. In the selling, explain the virtues of your new product or idea and resist the temptation to put down the competition. When you have expert confidence, you will be coming from a powerful position. Respect that power. If you do not, you will be humbled rather quickly. I don't want you to be a know-it-all. What I want is for you to have a depth of knowledge that is apparent when you speak so your words are well measured and meaningful.

Once you put your idea into motion, rarely will things go as you plan. Sometimes your timetable and the universe's timetable may not be in sync. But when you understand your subject from top to bottom, you will become very self-assured with the knowledge that you can handle any situation that comes your way.

In retrospect, if I had some of this knowledge earlier in my career, it would have been a lot easier for me. If you will do some of the things I suggest like networking (gaining and maintaining contacts), you can be more effective. Hard work isn't enough to get you where you want to be. There's more to success than the realization of a dream. I didn't value the people skills and knowledge base I needed to really make my career take off. I want you to be more prepared than I was and to have the tools available so you don't make the same mistakes I did.

How Do You Achieve Expert Confidence?

1. Be prepared by doing the necessary research. In sports broadcasting, I will use only 5% of the materials I have researched. Not knowing what will be needed, I will prepare for any and all eventualities. Then I can use the right information at the right time to be ready for whatever happens.
2. Recognize what 5% of the researched material to use and when. It's all about timing. Experience helps, but knowledge of the subject matter will enable you to have a great idea of what you should say and when you should say it. If I'm broadcasting a basketball game between Atlanta and Los Angeles, and I drop in a story about Boston, it would be out of place. It might show that I have great knowledge of the Celtics, but unless it was directly related to something happening in the game between Atlanta and LA, it would be forced and would not fit in that situation.
3. Be brave. With enough preparation, you can go into any situation unafraid. There is nothing that can happen that you cannot handle. One of my recurring

dreams (or I should say nightmares!) has me in a panic late for a game, missing a game, or showing up to broadcast a game with no notes or any preparation. Often, this dream will wake me up from what I thought was a sound sleep. I don't know why this dream keeps coming back to me, but it is a vivid reminder to always keep preparing, researching, and looking for new and better ways to communicate ideas.

4. Think creatively by using your newfound knowledge base to make connections you have never made before. As we did with our timeline, you will be amazed with the connections you can make between people, places, and events. One of the most underestimated activities that can help is to get quiet and think. Thinking time should be a part of your daily routine. So should meditation. Meditation need not always be about taking extra time out of your schedule. For example, air travel can be a hassle, but one of its benefits is the quiet time it affords. No phones. No Blackberries. Just you and your thoughts. Outdoor time is another example. Is there anything more wonderful than a summer's day, enjoying the outdoors with a good book? (Preferably in the shade!) Thinking and meditating on past events, connections, and space/time events (where I was and what I was doing) has been a well-spring for me. Ideas and possibilities come to me that I have never thought of before. There is magic in the quiet time. Let me shout it out, "MAKE TIME TO BE QUIET!"

5. Put yourself in a position where people come to you for expert advice on your subject. As a result, your

reputation and professional profile will increase. The story of Dr. Phil McGraw is a good example of one of those over-night success stories that took a couple of decades to make!

Born in Vinita, Oklahoma, to Jo and Jerry McGraw, Dr. Phil grew up in the oilfields of North Texas, where his father was an equipment supplier. Midway through his childhood, his family packed up and moved so that his father could pursue a lifelong dream of becoming a psychologist. McGraw attended high school at Shawnee Mission North High School in Mission, Kansas. He was given a football scholarship to attend the University of Tulsa but was injured and forced to transfer to Midwestern State University in Wichita Falls, Texas. McGraw graduated from the Midwestern State University in 1975 with a B.A. (Bachelor of Arts) in psychology, and then went on to get a Masters in experimental psychology and a Doctorate in clinical psychology at the University of North Texas.

McGraw owned a construction business with his brother-in-law while completing his residency. He did one-on-one sessions in private practice in Wichita Falls, Texas and conducted life skills seminars with his father before getting out of private practice and founding Courtroom Sciences, Inc., a trial consulting firm, in

1989. As president of CSI, he advised Fortune 500 companies as well as injured plaintiffs on how best to achieve settlements.

In 1995, Oprah Winfrey hired Phil McGraw to prepare her for the Amarillo Texas beef trial. Winfrey was so impressed with McGraw that she credited him for her victory in that case, which ended in 1998. Soon after, she invited him to appear on her show. His initial appearance proved so successful that he began appearing weekly as a "Relationship and Life Strategy Expert" on Tuesdays starting in April

1998. In 2002, he was given his own syndicated daily TV show, *Dr. Phil*, produced by Winfrey's Harpo Studios.

(copyright) Wikipedia-The Free Encyclopedia

6. Prepare for your success like it is a final exam for graduation or an Olympic event. Many hours go into really being ready to achieve your goal. When I used to anchor TV sports for WTKR-TV in Norfolk, Virginia, I was given 3-4 minutes in the newscast for the nightly sports report. And on average, it took me one hour to write and produce one minute of television. So, a 4 minute sportscast would take me 4 hours to prepare. I did this sportscast three times a day for the 5 p.m., 6 p.m. and 11 p.m. news. So I was generally either at the station or at home preparing 12 hours a day for 12 minutes on the air.

When you are doing your research, don't just look in books, magazines, and other printed materials but also consider audio and video resources as well. Take notes. If you don't have a digital voice recorder app on your phone, consider getting one. You have to capture ideas as they come because they are fleeting, and you might not ever think of them again.

The internet is also an excellent tool for research. One tool I use is Google Alert. This allows you to get the latest information on any topic using a process where it scans newspapers, blogs, etc. and then Google emails this information to you.

In this digital age, the apps on your iPhone or Android will be very beneficial. The information gets to you quickly, but, because of space limitations, it is very limited in depth. But this information, by the sheer speed of delivery, is beneficial. But for the purpose of YOU gaining Expert Confidence, better do to your research on line first, and then by establishing relationships with others.

Expert Confidence Exercise #1

Organize the materials you have researched. We talked about Bill Parcells in Chapter 4. The timeline can be broken down into three categories: key people, important events, and final outcomes. Use the following chart to break down your timeline into these three categories.

KEY PEOPLE	IMPORTANT EVENTS	FINAL OUTCOMES
Example Bill Parcells	*Won Two Super Bowls*	*Recognized as one of pro football's greatest coaches*
Ray Perkins, Head Coach of the New York Giants	*Hired Bill as assistant*	*Started Parcells' path to him becoming the team's head coach*

Expert Confidence Exercise #2

Your research will distill the information into a few key points. Write what you think those points are.

_____

_____

_____

_____

_____

_____

Expert Confidence Exercise #3

Based on your research, write down any anecdotes or stories you think are important.

_____

_____

_____

_____

_____

_____

_____

_____

_____

Expert Confidence Exercise #4

Create a filing system for the information you have collected with a code that makes sense to you. You can do this on your computer or on notebook paper or whatever other method that works best for you. It is important to make sure you have an easy way of finding this information again when you need it.

Included following this page is a copy of one of my NBA score sheets and is what I work off of to broadcast the game. It contains all of the information that I need at my fingertips. This is from a game between the Atlanta Hawks and the Los Angeles Lakers. This game was played at the Staples Center in Los Angeles, California on February 15, 2006. The Hawks info is on the left, and the Lakers on the right.

The CAREER box you see in the upper left hand corner is the Hawks all-time and single- game record holders in points, rebounds, and assists. In case we have a record broken in these areas, I have it handy and don't have to look it up while the game is going on.

(The Hawks record for most points by a player in a game is 57, held jointly by

Dominique Wilkins (NIQUE), Bob Pettit, and Lou Hudson.)

Next, you'll see the players listed. The starters occupy the first five slots and then the subs are listed.

You'll find, in red, #1 Josh Childress. I made special mention of Josh in the broadcast because he is an LA native. I talked about his high school career and college experience at Stanford.

All of those numbers to the right of the player are his season stats, his season and career highs. The others' numbers, (check Kobe Bryant #8 in purple on the right) 5, 7, 10, 13, 15 etc. This is his running point total. I keep my own score during the game.

I mentioned to you briefly about when to use info. Look near the bottom of the Hawks column. Do you see where it says Marc Stern of Malibu? If it fit, I was going to share the story of this gentleman. Mr. Stern attended Dickinson College in Pennsylvania. As an 18- year-old sophomore, he had a ticket to go see an NBA game in Hershey, Pennsylvania between the Knicks and the Philadelphia Warriors on March 2, 1962. But he opted to stay at school and study for an exam instead of going to the game. That night, Wilt Chamberlain set the all-time single-game scoring record in the NBA when he scored 100 points!

Well, Mr. Stern is now a Lakers season ticket holder. He held a ticket for a Lakers- Toronto game at Staples Center on January 22, 2006. But he didn't make it. A family birthday party was scheduled for the same day, and he gave his tickets away. That night, the Lakers Kobe Bryant scored 81 points, the second highest point total in league history! So Mr. Stern held tickets to the 2 highest scoring games by an individual in NBA history and attended neither! That is a remarkable story to me. But we had to pick the right time and place to use it. It took us a while, but we did show Mr. Stern and shared his story.

This is the kind of preparation that I'm asking you to undertake in your own style and with your own system, of course. But you need to have complete knowledge at your fingertips, so you can use it on a moment's notice. That is Expert Confidence!

Expert Confidence Exercise #5

After you have done the research, you should write down some things you now know that the average person would not know. These are the things that make you an expert.

_____

_____

_____

_____

_____

_____

_____

_____

_____

_____

_____

_____

_____

_____

_____

_____

_____

_____

"When you know a thing, to hold that you know it, and when you do not know a thing, to allow that you do not know it - this is knowledge."
- Confucius

"Those people who develop the ability to continuously acquire new and better forms of knowledge that they can apply to their work and to their lives will be the movers and shakers in our society for the indefinite future."
- Brian Tracy

Chapter 5

20-Second Time Out

Each team is entitled to one (1) 20-second timeout per half and each overtime period. During a 20-second timeout, both teams shall have unlimited legal substitutions.
- Official rules of the National Basketball Association

20-Second Time Out

What Is A 20-Second Time Out?

In professional basketball, a 20-second timeout is used by a team to make a quick change in the flow of the game. Not as dramatic as a full timeout, these brief stoppages can reverse unfavorable momentum or set up a strategy for a score. These timeouts allow a team to evaluate what is happening at the moment and make a mid-course correction.

It's time now for us to utilize a 20-second time out in the Fast Forward Winner^{TM} Program. What follows in this chapter will help determine how you are progressing and if you need to make any course corrections. The tools mentioned here are especially helpful if things aren't going 100% your way because you can use them before you get discouraged. Without this honest self-feedback, you will not be able to rise to the top.

Why Is A 20-Second Time Out Important?

Even if you lived the perfect life up until now (went to church every Sunday, helped little old ladies across the street, bought every last Girl Scout cookie), there is a pretty good chance that something unforeseen is going to happen to you during the pursuit of your dream. Having the tools you need at your disposal will help you get through any tough times you might experience.

Bad things happen to good people. Even when you think you are on the perfect course, things might not line up the way you envision. This is the time to take what you've done so far and determine what has and hasn't worked. Now is when you should make some adjustments to get back on track to the destination you want to reach. If success isn't happening for you, determine the reason things aren't going the way you want and make some changes.

What Are The Steps For Taking A 20-Second Timeout?

There are two sides to analyze in a 20-second timeout. One is the proactive side and the other is the reactive side. The proactive side addresses the positive things you are doing to achieve your goals while the reactive side looks at how you are responding to situations or obstacles you might be encountering.

Proactive:

1. Make sure you've done all you can do. Have you decided on a goal, done the research, and interviewed experts to get feedback so you can make your dream happen? You need to determine if you have maintained your commitment by doing the things you said you would do like making phone calls, sending emails, making appointments, etc. Have you been true to your word?

2. Have you been true to your reading and research goals? If you said you were going to read a book a week to become an expert in this field, have you done that? Don't make a goal or say you're going to do something if you're not going to follow through. You want to make sure you are taking proactive steps and doing all you said you would do. If you say you're going to do something and don't, you are

sending mixed messages about what you really want and whether you are really committed to your goal.

3. Ask yourself this question: "How are my people skills?" Whether or not you are a friendly person is one of the biggest factors in determining your success, whether it's a job interview, a relationship, or undertaking your dream. You have to be someone other people want to be around. If you are around a whiner/complainer, how do you react to that? You don't want to be around them. They bring you down and are roadblocks to be avoided. On the other hand, when you are around someone who gets you excited, who you have fun with, and who you like, you get more done because you enjoy being with this person.

Everything we get in life is a shared responsibility. No man is an island. You want to be around positive people who share, not negative people who don't. You want to be a both a giver and a receiver. If you think you are a shy, reserved person or feel like you have trouble making friends, by all means, stop this course right now and go work on this area of your life. There is nothing that is going to affect your future more than your personality and people skills.

Reactive:

1. Follow through. Just because somebody doesn't get back in touch with you doesn't mean that they are going to tell you "no" or that they are not going to be cooperative. It's okay to ask again. It's very appropriate to follow up.

As you reach out to people you don't know, promote yourself to others as someone who is going to respond quickly. Immediate return of phone calls or emails is crucial. Don't let any communication or correspondence someone sends to you go unanswered. This is especially important when you are making contacts and can make or break a fledgling business.

2. Be creative. Think outside the box. Try to make contacts in "off-the-chart" kinds of ways, especially if you aren't getting follow-up from the other side. Michael Michalko has written two books: *Cracking Creativity* and *Thinker Toys*. They both are designed to help you think and say things in different ways and to look at things from a unique perspective. The point is that utilizing creative thinking will help you if you find conventional means are not getting the job done. It will help you to think of original ways to accomplish various tasks (i.e. if you are a writer, you could send your script in a trashcan since that's where it's probably going to end up anyway). It could be a simple thing like sending a package FedEx instead of using the regular U.S. Postal Service. You could also develop either an audio or video email rather than a regular, typed email. Here is where some work on yourself is helpful to get you to think more creatively. One thing I did to promote my speaking business was to format my business card in the form of a baseball card. It's a unique idea that gets people to remember me. Use humor. It's a good way to get you noticed and will help you stand out from crowd.

3. Send out your best work: All correspondence should be well-written (grammatically correct, properly

punctuated, correctly spelled, etc.). If you feel like this is an area you are deficient in, by all means, get some help. And if you don't know whether or not you're deficient, contact a professional and ask him/her for an honest evaluation of your writing.

When you are evaluating your proactive and reactive progress thus far, you should be aware that the need for course corrections is necessary in pretty much any endeavor. In fact, they were commonplace during all the Apollo space flights.

Were you aware that you could not fly straight to the moon? If you are old enough to remember the Apollo space flights, you might recall a series of 'mid-course' corrections that were necessary to keep the lunar module on course for its target.

Here's part of the actual transcript from the Apollo 8 mission's flight journal:

Public Affairs Officer - "This is Apollo Control at 58 hours into the flight of Apollo 8. We've had no communications with the spacecraft since our last report, and here in Mission Control it has also been rather quiet. At the present time, the spacecraft is at an altitude of 28,225 nautical miles from the Moon and velocity reads 4,024 feet per second. Coming up, in just a little under 3 hours, we have a midcourse correction maneuver scheduled. This is listed as midcourse correction number 4 in the Flight Plan and will actually be the second midcourse correction on route to the Moon. Midcourse corrections 2 and 3, which were listed in the Flight Plan, were such low values that they were not performed, and we anticipate that midcourse correction coming up will be for about 3 feet per second, a burn of about 3 feet per second using the spacecraft Reaction Control System. At 58 hours, 1 minute; this is Apollo Control."

http://history.nasa.gov/ap08fj/10day3_maroon.htm

To accomplish great things, especially things that have never been done before, you must "shoot for the moon" and constantly evaluate your progress, making any necessary course corrections along the way in order to reach your goal.

20-Second Timeout Exercise #1

Go back to Exercise 1 from Chapter 2 on page 21. Make a chart of what you said you would do, what you did, and what the result was.

PROMISE	ACTION	RESULT
Example: Committed to a career in sports broadcasting.	Enrolled in Catawba College's Speech program. Earned a B.A. degree in speech	. Learned how to use voice, speech, range—all the tools for a career in speaking.

After completing the chart, answer the following questions, using commitment and affirmation statements about things like following up on emails. Write down some different ways of getting the desired results. Of those actions I took, can I break them down into the 6 proactive and reactive steps mentioned earlier in this chapter? Explain.

_____

_____

_____

_____

_____

Did I do what I said I was going to do? Explain.

_____

_____

_____

_____

_____

Did I prepare like I said I would? Explain.

_____

_____

_____

_____

_____

If I didn't, what changes do I need to make to my daily routine to make this happen? Am I going to get up an hour earlier or stay up an hour later? Can I break the task down where it can be completed in three 20 minute time segments throughout the day?

_____
_____
_____
_____
_____
_____
_____
_____
_____
_____
_____
_____
_____
_____
_____
_____
_____
_____

What am I doing in terms of developing my people skills?

_____
_____
_____
_____

How has my follow-through been?

_____
_____
_____
_____

No matter who you are or what you do, there will be others who criticize you, especially if you are in the public eye like I am. I know it's hard to believe, but not everyone thinks I'm the world's greatest sportscaster! And for someone who gets his feelings hurt easily, it can be a painful exercise to venture forth into the marketplace with a new idea or performance and see your good name smeared all over the place. Even if your dream might not attract public venom, there will come a time when you will need to step out and stand up for what you believe in. And that brings us to courage.

Whatever you do, you need courage. Whatever course you decide upon, there is always someone to tell you that you are wrong. There are always difficulties arising that tempt you to believe your critics are right. To map out a course of action and follow it to an end requires some of the same courage that a soldier needs. Peace has its victories, but it takes brave men and women to win them.
- Ralph Waldo Emerson

I don't have a magic potion, or a personal story, to help you through this. You just have to step out and put your faith to the test. If a seed has been planted in you to do something worthwhile with your life (and it has), then now is the time to complete the mission. Make your mid-course corrections. Know you are on the right path.

It is not the critic who counts, not the man who points out how the strong man stumbled, or where the doer of deeds could have done better. The credit belongs to the man who is actually in the arena, whose face is marred by dust and sweat and blood, who strives valiantly, who errs and comes short again and again, who knows the great enthusiasms, the great devotions, and spends himself in a worthy cause, who at best knows achievement and who at the worst if he fails at least fails while daring greatly so that his place shall never be with those cold and timid souls who know neither victory nor defeat.

- *Theodore Roosevelt*

It's always been tough for me to take rejection well. I had it in my brain that if I worked hard and was a good person, naturally, things would fall my way. The world doesn't work like that. If I had it to do all over again, I would make the following changes in my programmed way of looking at the world. (These are lessons I hope to instill in my children).

- Be clear about what it is you want.
- Eliminate ALL negative thoughts.
- Think only about what you want, in positive terms. When the negative emotions come, that is an alarm going off telling you that something is not right. Make changes immediately! At all times, go only for what you want, not what you don't want. It is your creation. Plan it well.

- Do what is right for YOU. Don't rely on others. Example: Should I call this lady or not? If your intuition says yes, CALL! If it doesn't, DON'T.
- Recognize that the path you are on is yours and yours alone. Try to avoid comparisons to others. This is incredibly hard in this American celebrity culture.
- Strive to stay true to your beliefs.
- Be tough in the marketplace. Present yourself as how you want to be remembered. Be a class act. You will run into some real dirt bags and lowlifes. These are the people who will teach you the most. Until you pass that internal test, they will keep showing up.
- Just remember that the good news is that there are more people who want to help you than want to hurt you.
- Also remember when you affirm your goals and take action, you've enlisted the help of the universe in making your dreams come true. When you make positive choices and analyze the results, the universe is arranging circumstances on a metaphysical plane. You have to trust that everything is working out in divine order

Chapter 6

Curved Bat

"Don't let the fear of striking out hold you back. Every strike brings me closer to the next home run."
- Babe Ruth

Curved Bat

What Is A Curved Bat?

It's the tool you need to hit the curve balls life throws at you. Most major league hitters have no problem hitting a fast ball because it is straight, and they can see it coming. Curve balls, however, are much trickier to hit. You have to anticipate them and practice hitting them. The joke is that the only way anyone can hit a curve ball squarely is with a curved bat. Your preparation and your ability to think creatively are two of the main features of your curved bat, helping you deal with the problems that come your way.

Why Is A Having A Curved Bat Important?

I want to load up your toolbox with all the necessary implements to make your dreams come true. And since there is no such thing in baseball as a "curved bat" let's imagine it and put it to good use! Your "curved bat" helps you survive all the unexpected events which occur in both your business and your life. It is one thing to swing at and miss a curve. That would be like putting out your best proposal that's been OK'd at every level of an organization, only to be shot down at the last minute. But what about the curve ball that hits you right in the ribs? Some examples would include losing your job or getting divorced.

When misfortunes come your way, don't do what I did (i.e. lose your temper, withdraw from people, etc.). You need to come up with different and better ways of solving your problems (i.e. the curved bat). Here is where you have to dig deep inside yourself to see what you are made of. Major league curve balls force you to get into character issues of what to do when things go wrong.

I have a lot of issues with competition, anger, etc., especially when a team I am covering is playing beneath its standards. It's so obvious to me that a slight mental adjustment might save the entire game; instead, the team makes the same mistake over and over again, turning it into one HUGE mistake. As a result, more often than not, the team's entire season is ruined, causing coaches to be fired and players to be traded. When you feel like you're on the short end of the stick, it's tough. What you decide to do affects a lot of people. It's so true the saying that "sports do not build character, they reveal it."

Are you faced with a decision on going to college? Graduate School? Getting into the college of your choice can be one of the most stressful events of your life. If your heart is set on going to one specific school, you will know what it takes to get in very clearly. Then, it's up to the admissions office. And if they say no, here's my advice: where you go is not that important to your future success. Unless you want to study a specific discipline and need that degree from a certain college or university, where you go is not that big a deal. In general terms, where you go pales in comparison to what you do once you get in. This is a critical distinction that will save you a ton of stress.

Once inside those ivy-covered walls, get going! That is where the information included in Fast Forward WinnerTM can really help. Since you or someone else (family, friends, scholarships) is now paying for the privilege of education, it is up to you to get FROM the school the tips, the training, and contacts to make your dreams come true.

College is where you can really begin to build relationships that will pay off for a lifetime. But this will not happen if you do not take the initiative. Be a leader. Ask questions. Volunteer. There will be plenty of time to hang out, party, and enjoy your college experience. But you have to be a student first: a student that is dedicated to getting the most for your money so you can launch yourself into the market place as someone special.

You have to come up with a set of tools that will allow you not to make big mistakes. You need this chapter to help you deal with all the things that can occur which are beyond your control, which may be interpreted as setbacks.

What Are The Steps For Creating A Curved Bat?

Get control of your anger. It's important not to lash out at others even if you're right and they're wrong. Bite your tongue. Speaking from personal experience, that's something hard for a broadcaster to do.

One of the most devastating curve balls that I have been thrown in my career was in the summer of 2004. My contract to broadcast the Hawks games was up (I had an option year for 2004-05). I thought it would be a mere formality because all of the feedback I had received from my employer had been positive, and the team was solidly in my corner. Well, unbeknownst to the team and me, this employer had been talking with another announcer about taking over my play-by-play duties. So when the time came to exercise my option, they chose to let me go instead.

I was stunned. I lost 2/3 of my income, along with my family's health insurance and other benefits. I was so angry that I violated all of the things I'm going to insist you do! (How's that for being a great teacher?) Sadly, my ego got in the way. I thought I would be looked at in my industry as some dumb klutz who got dumped, never to return. Of course, that was not the case. The team, and the rest of the NBA, knew what had happened, realized what a mistake had been made, and now, a decade later, I have my full time job back broadcasting Hawks games for Fox Sports South. I am proud to report that my loyalty to Fox and the Hawks was rewarded. Both I and my family have been blessed. So, all that said, I hope you will remember these points:

1. Stay on purpose and amp up instead of withdrawing. I have a tendency to withdraw when things go wrong, to lock down and not associate with people. Instead of going into a shell, you should increase your visibility and communication with others. I learned this from author/speaker Andy Andrews: the only way that we are going to ultimately get ahead in this world is with the help of other people. If you are warm-hearted and friendly, you will attract others in a positive way, and relationships start to build. If you withdraw in tough times, people will not be drawn to you; in fact, they will shun you because you will have turned into a bitter, mean-spirited, down-in-the-dumps person that no one wants to be around. When that happens, relationships break down, and the help-chain of human interaction gets broken.

2. Broaden your dream. For example, if your goal is to be a player in the NBA, you have to know that

despite your best efforts, the odds are very low of making it. There are millions of kids who play basketball, and there are only 30 teams with 15 players per team, so in the NBA, there are 450 player jobs available. That's pretty select company. But there are hundreds of ways to be involved in the NBA. The Atlanta Spirit as a company has approximately 300 employees, but only 15 of those 300 are basketball players. The remaining 285 Atlanta Spirit employees are still working in the NBA. They might not be playing, but their involvement in the success of the franchise is just as significant as the players, and in some cases, more so. I want you to dream about being in the NBA, but I want you to broaden that dream and look not just at chances to play the game but for other opportunities like in ticketing, coaching, community development, etc. If you get into any of these areas, you will still have reached your dream.

3. Use a positive attitude to ultimately win the day. A lot of people downplay the importance of being positive. Americans have been so conditioned through newspapers, television, and other media to always hear all the bad things that are happening in the world (rapes, kidnappings, deaths, etc.) that they often don't think about concentrating on the good things going on in the world instead. If you think that you're not as positive as you need to be, then you should take action to get this reinforced. One thing you can do, as speaker/author Brian Tracy suggests, is to use that first hour of your day, when you arise, to read positive and inspirational books and stories. Instead of grabbing the newspaper and

reading all the terrible news of the past 24 hours, pick up a piece of inspirational literature. Use that first "Golden Hour" to set the tone of your day. As you drive into work or school, turn off the radio, and instead, program your brain by listening to great speakers with words of inspiration and hope. I do this routinely. I never watch TV in the morning. I will get the newspaper out of the driveway, but ALWAYS go to the Sports page, never the front page (I just have to know the scores!!). But I never listen to talk radio, sports talk radio, or anything else driving in the morning. I have my iPod locked and loaded with great podcasts and CDs of great speakers that I can listen to in the car, when I exercise, or as I travel. This is a must for me — make it a must for you.

4. Choose your words carefully because they have great impact and meaning. Words are powerful. Negative words are especially hurtful. You want to avoid saying negative things to others. Think about it. Do you work well when someone is screaming at you? If you don't like to be yelled at, what makes you think other people will respond positively to you yelling at them? Instead, when you want to make a point, change your voice pattern (tone, volume, etc.). That change will get people's attention without causing any negative energy between you.

In trying to hit the curve balls in life, there are some key strategies to always keep in mind no matter what.

• Curve balls are easy to hit if you know they are coming. The reason they throw hitters off is because they are looking for another pitch like the fast ball instead. So how do you hit an unexpected curve ball? You have to anticipate that you're going to be thrown curve balls and have a backup plan.

- Don't let a curve ball throw you off your game. Challenging situations come, and they go. Just remember, "This too shall pass." You've got to remain in the flow of your game so you can stay on course and on track.
- There are many examples in baseball of players who weren't given much of a chance but stayed on purpose with a never-give-up attitude. One of the great stories is that of catcher Mike Piazza. Who would have thought that a guy that was picked in the 62nd round of the draft would go on to become the National League's Rookie of the Year, and eventually, the top-hitting catcher in the history of baseball? Mike Piazza beat the odds and proved the naysayers (who speculated he was selected due to his family's friendship with Dodgers manager Tommy Lasorda), wrong.

Piazza vowed to learn to catch if he was drafted, and his power hitting led him to becoming a perennial All-Star baseball player. He recorded his best overall offensive year in 1997, his final full season with the L.A. Dodgers, hitting .362 and notching 124 runs batted in. He also became only the third catcher ever to hit 40 home runs in a season that golden year. There are different ways of dealing with life's curve balls. Here's one that always makes me smile.

In the movie *Major League*, (1989) the character Pedro Cerrano (played by Dennis Haysbert) becomes superstitious about his inability to hit a curve ball: In this scene, Lou Brown, the manager, and Duke Temple, a coach on the team, are discussing Cerrano's hitting ability.

PEDRO CERRANO

(In the batting cage, knocking the cover off pitch after pitch with his black bat.)

BROWN

Jesus, this guy hits a ton. How come nobody else picked up on him?

TEMPLE

(To the batting practice pitcher, Harris)

Okay, Harris, that's enough fast balls. Throw some curves.

(Harris winds and throws a fair-to-middlin' curve ball. Cerrano swings and misses it a foot)

BROWN

Oh!

(Later in the movie)

(35-year-old former player, JAKE TAYLOR who is now making a comeback is talking with Carrano. Taylor is undressing, but his attention is diverted by Cerrano whose stall is right next to him. Cerrano has set up an altar in his locker. In front of his bats, which are lined up like sentinels, is a table covered with pictures of baseball players, figurines of saints, several lit candles and, in the middle, a primitive fetish doll with a cigar in its mouth. Cerrano has drawn some magic signs on his bats. He finishes an incantation and then lights the cigar on the fetish doll. In the clubhouse are players Willie Mays Hayes and Eddie Harris)

TAYLOR

What are you doin' there, Pedro?

CERRANO

Bats. They are sick.

TAYLOR

So are mine. Is somethin' goin' around?

CERRANO

No hit curve ball. Straight ball, hit it very much. Curve ball, bats are afraid. I ask Jo-Buu to come. Take fear from bats.

HAYES

Jo-Buu?

TAYLOR

Maybe he's the pagan saint of baseball.

CERRANO

I offer him cigars and gin. He will come.

(Cerrano pours some gin in a small cup and puts it next to the fetish doll. Harris has been listening to all this. Cerrano grabs a towel to head for the showers)

HARRIS

I wouldn't leave this gin sittin' around out here with this group.

CERRANO

(With a certain gravity)

Is very bad to steal Jo-Buu's gin. Is very bad.

(Cerrano closes his locker and goes off to the showers, leaving everyone to wonder just how bad this team will be)

Curve balls can make you look really bad when you don't know they are coming. Don't panic. You are not going to die if you swing and miss a curve ball that comes your way.

Your career is not going to be over. Lots of people have been thrown curve balls before and survived them. The game will continue even if you strike out this time. Try to keep a sense of humor and not be embarrassed about the situation. Things happen. Move on and realize that even the best hitters strike out on a regular basis.

Before the Curve Ball comes, cultivate your resources by staying in touch with people: friends, contacts, networks, etc. and treat everyone you know with dignity and respect. Be a giver so that when it's your time to be on the receiving end, you will have more credit than debits. Then when a curve ball comes, and you find yourself leaning on people, they will be happy to help you.

The way you handle your curved bat (your unique perspective on life) could serve as your selling point. You may find that no matter what comes your way, you have an unconventional tool you can use just in case. Lance Armstrong is an example of someone who, with his combination of mental toughness and being used as a guinea pig, gives a whole new slant to recovery from cancer. Your unique slant may be the breakthrough the world needs. We've all read stories about people who have used misfortune as a turning point in their lives, whether it was something physical like Olympian Steven Holcomb or a business breakthrough like Bernie Marcus at Home Depot.

Holcomb is the captain of adversity. He overcame degenerative eye disease with a surgical procedure in 2008 and has gone on to win bobsled medals at Vancouver in 2010 and Sochi in 2014. The surgery restored his vision from 20-500 to 20-20. Holcomb blasted his way through a calf injury in February 2014 to claim a bronze medal in the two-man bobsled, the first United States medal in that event in 62-years!

Marcus was born to Jewish-Russian immigrant parents in Newark, New Jersey. He grew up in a tenement and wanted to become a doctor. He couldn't afford the tuition, so he worked for his father as a cabinet maker while attending school at Rutgers University to earn a pharmacy degree.

Later, he worked at a drugstore as a druggist but became more interested in the business and retailing side of the industry. He worked at a cosmetics company and various other retail jobs, eventually reaching a position as a top executive with Handy Dan Improvement Centers, a Los Angeles-based chain of home improvement stores. In 1978, after a disagreement with his boss at Handy Dan, he and Home Depot co-founder Arthur Blank were both fired.

Together, with the help of New York investment banker Ken Langone, who assembled a group of investors, the two launched the highly successful home-improvement retailer, Home Depot, in 1979. The store revolutionized the home improvement business with its warehouse concept, and both Marcus and Blank became billionaires as a result.

© Wikipedia

Marcus took the misfortune that was dealt to him, and not only did he succeed on a personal basis, but he also succeeded on a commercial level to such a remarkable extent that the rest of the world wants to know how he did it. Your story might be so incredible that we'll be writing books about you too. I always remember a line from Deepak Chopra: "If anybody has ever done it in the past, you can too."

One of the most heroic baseball stories of all time centers around Lou Gehrig. Known as the "Iron Horse" because of his number of consecutive-games streak, Gehrig was beloved because of the way he handled an incredible personal crisis.

In 1938, Gehrig fell below .300 in batting average for the first time since 1925, and it was clear that there was something wrong. He lacked his usual strength. Pitches he would have hit for homeruns were only fly outs.

Gehrig played the first eight games of the 1939 season, but he managed only four hits. On a ball he hit back to pitcher Johnny Murphy, Gehrig had trouble getting to first base.

When he returned to the dugout, his teammates complimented him on the "good play." Gehrig knew when his fellow Yankees had to congratulate him for stumbling out of the batter's box and up the first base line, it was time to leave baseball. So he took himself out of the game. On May 2, 1939, as Yankee captain, he took the lineup card to the umpires, as usual. But his name was not on the roster. Instead, Babe Dahlgren was stationed at first. The game announcer remarked, "Ladies and gentlemen, Lou Gehrig's consecutive streak of 2,130 games played has ended."

Doctors at the Mayo Clinic diagnosed Gehrig with a very rare form of a degenerative disease: amyotrophic lateral sclerosis (ALS), which is now called Lou Gehrig's disease. There was no chance he would ever play baseball again. When he retired, Lou gave a speech that will live forever. It was one of the most poignant and emotional moments in the history of American sports:

"Fans, for the past two weeks you have been reading about the bad break I got. Yet today

I consider myself the luckiest man on the face of this earth. I have been in ballparks for seventeen years and have never received anything but kindness and encouragement from you fans.

Look at these grand men. Which of you wouldn't consider it the highlight of his career just to associate with them for even one day? Sure, I'm lucky....

When you have a wonderful mother-in-law who takes sides with you in squabbles with her own daughter - that's something. When you have a father and a mother who work all their lives so you can have an education and build your body - it's a blessing. When you have a wife who has been a tower of strength and shown more courage than you dreamed existed - that's the finest I know.

So I close in saying that I may have had a tough break, but I have an awful lot to live for."

- From the Official Lou Gehrig website.

Curved Bat Exercise #1

Think back to a major league curve ball (unexpected event) you were thrown either in your school or personal life.

What happened?

_____
_____
_____
_____
_____
_____
_____
_____
_____
_____
_____
_____
_____
_____

How did you react initially?

_____
_____
_____
_____
_____
_____
_____

What was the result?

_____

_____

_____

_____

_____

_____

_____

_____

If you had it to do over, what would you have done differently?

_____

_____

_____

_____

_____

_____

_____

_____

_____

_____

_____

_____

What was the wisdom that lesson was trying to teach you?

_____

_____

_____

_____

_____

_____

_____

_____

_____

_____

_____

_____

_____

_____

Curve balls are coming. The universe will keep testing you and your resolve until you figure it out. Unexpected occurrences will come in different forms and different fashions; you need to know you can handle them based on your past experiences. Determine how you will react (not yell and scream but stay calm and think about what to do next).

This section may cause you to draw on some emotions that you have had buried for years. Let them come out and release them. The purpose of this exercise is to recognize what you did in the past, analyze it, and put together a plan so that you handle it better in the future. We're assuming for the point of this discussion, that you may not have handled a particular curve ball in your past with your personal best. Use this time now to pre-pave the road you wish to follow in the future. Recognize a potential curve ball and visualize the way you want it to go in your favor. See a positive result. Focus on that outcome.

Curved Bat Exercise #2

One way to gauge your reactions in challenging situations is to determine whether you normally react to situations positively or negatively. Each day for a week keep a journal where you write down both the positive and negative things you say and think. At the end of the week see which list is longer so you can really look at whether you react positively or negatively most of the time.

Event	Positive	Negative
A graphic on the screen says the Hawks have missed their last 10 shots when they have only missed their last 7.	*Ignore it or say something like: "I believe that streak is only 7 missed shots. Let's double check that." (This gives them a chance to go back and fix it.)*	Throw people who made the mistake under the bus by saying something like: "That's not right. They've only missed 7 shots. 0 and 7 is bad enough. Come on, guys, get it together."

I've asked a lot of you with these exercises. I've used examples of some pretty famous people who have attained world-class status. But what about you and me? Our challenges come in all shapes and sizes. No matter where we are in life, the next opportunity to grow and to change is seconds away: the friend you haven't spoken to in a while, a neighbor who has just been let go at work, your daughter who is struggling with her homework assignment, your spouse who is sad because this is the day that her mom passed away. Have your antenna up. Curve balls are all around us. Now is the time to be proactive and start hitting those pitches out of the park.

There is an old saying that I remember about church pastors. It went something like: "Preachers preach best when discussing their own sins." And I feel a little bit like that as we come to the end of our time together. What I have asked you to do in this journey are tasks that, yes, I have done, but also need to work on constantly.

Since I started writing this, two significant events have transpired in my professional life. First, I had my baseball job taken away from me. Oh, I knew the day was coming. With the overlap of two major league professional sports seasons, the NBA and Major League Baseball, there was no way that I could continue in both worlds simultaneously. So, I've had to deal with the fact that for the first time since 1987, I do not broadcast major league baseball anymore. Because it is a desire of mine to continue in broadcasting baseball in some fashion, I will take my own advice and come up with a way to make it happen. I will start with the Seed Dream and then take the actions necessary to make my dream a reality again. Right now I am in the middle of a 20-second time out practicing with my curved bat to prepare for any difficulties which might arise. I already have the expert confidence that comes with experience.

On the basketball front, now my full time career, the team I broadcast for is going through leadership changes in the front office and on its roster. So I have to remember to keep things positive and think about what I want instead of what I don't want when it comes to broadcasting the games. I know I need to stay upbeat for the viewers and fans.

As you step out on your journey, know that I'm your fan, someone in the stands cheering you on, not someone broadcasting to you what to do. Nothing would please me more than to hear about your success story one day when your great hope and desire turns into an achieved goal.

Stay in touch with me if you wish. My contact information is included here. If Atlanta is in your city playing NBA basketball, I'm probably there, near the scorer's table, working on my ad libs. I'd love to meet you, either at a game or at one of my speaking events.

Good luck, not that you'll need any. Since you have already taken the first step toward becoming a Fast Forward Winner, luck is already on your side.

BOB RATHBUN
PROFESSIONAL SPEAKER & EMMY-AWARD WINNING BROADCASTER

Bob Rathbun's broadcast career started at the ripe old age of 12 when he was asked to broadcast a half-inning of an American Legion baseball game. And he hasn't stopped since!

Since that night at Newman Park in Salisbury, North Carolina, Bob has gone on to become one of the most respected and popular sports broadcasters in the country.

Annually, Bob broadcasts well over 100 games and events. He is the signature voice of Fox Sports Network South, handling the network's play- by-play responsibilities for the NBA Atlanta Hawks and the WNBA Atlanta Dream. He announces numerous college football, basketball, and baseball games for FSN South and SportSouth. Bob served as the network's play-by- play voice for the Atlanta Braves from 1997 to 2006.

Bob is also back for his 27th season calling the action for Atlantic Coast Conference basketball on the Raycom Sports Network. An eight-time state sportscaster of the year in Virginia and Georgia, Bob has garnered nine Emmy awards for his broadcasting excellence, and in April, 2006, Bob was named to the Catawba College Sports Hall of Fame. In 2004, Bob expanded his work into the realm of motivation, leadership, and team building when he joined John Maxwell's Maximum Impact Club as a host and speaker. Bob is also a past host of Nightingale-Conant's *Success Streams* audio series. Now, Bob has taken what he has learned as an announcer and interviewer and put it all together as a keynote speaker, Emcee and lecturer.

Bob lives in the Atlanta area with his wife, Marybeth, and his two children, Court and Grace.

Bob's Suggested Books, Audios, And Videos

The Law of Attraction –Esther and Jerry Hicks
https://amzn.to/2S04iYs

First, Break All the Rules – Marcus Buckingham and Curt W. Coffman
https://amzn.to/2CRyzEx

The Spirit to Serve – J. W. Marriott and Kathi Ann Brown
https://amzn.to/2CWMb1g

Thinking for a Change – John C. Maxwell
https://amzn.to/2EFUNey

Failing Forward – John C. Maxwell
https://amzn.to/2CquZQB

The Generosity Factor – Ken Blanchard and S. Truett Cathy
https://amzn.to/2S0txtK

The Power of Focus – Mark Victor Hansen, Jack Canfield and Les Hewitt
https://amzn.to/2RXWI0B

Your Road Map for Success – John C. Maxwell
https://amzn.to/2RZD1W3

Developing the Leader Within You – John C. Maxwell
https://amzn.to/2q1Gc2K

The 5 Patterns of Extraordinary Careers – James M. Citrin and Richard Smith
https://amzn.to/2Cq9T54

The Fred Factor - Mark Sanborn
https://amzn.to/2Eykeyq

Today Matters - John C. Maxwell
https://amzn.to/2NNaSOH

Habit: From Effectiveness to Greatness - Stephen R. Covey
https://amzn.to/2RW25NA

Who Moved My Cheese - Spencer Johnson
https://amzn.to/2CRfbaB

Pour Your Heart Into It - Howard Schultz and Dori Jones Yang
https://amzn.to/2CrNt3c

The World is Flat - Thomas Friedman
https://amzn.to/2CqwUEN

First Things First - Stephen R. Covey
https://amzn.to/2S0AAma

The Traveler's Gift - Andy Andrews
https://amzn.to/2CrNUur

Island of Saints - Andy Andrews
https://amzn.to/2CRAclD

Lost Choice - Andy Andrews
https://amzn.to/2pYz6fd

Love is the Killer App - Tim Sanders
https://amzn.to/2CswYnF

The Likeability Factor - Tim Sanders
https://amzn.to/2CtL1JM

Goals! - Brian Tracy
https://amzn.to/2S0EKKD

Turbo Coach - Brian Tracy and Campbell Fraser
https://amzn.to/2EykQ7k

Manifest Your Destiny - Wayne Dyer
https://amzn.to/2CU1eJ5

One Piece of Paper – Mike Figliuolo
https://amzn.to/2yMAWE2

You Let Some Girl Beat You? – Ann Meyers Drysdale
https://amzn.to/2CpA7od

Power – Jeffrey Pfeffer
https://amzn.to/2CSAt7F

The Book of Afformations® -Noah St. John
https://amzn.to/2pZu8iv

The Power of Why – C. Richard Weylman

https://amzn.to/2CqydUd

Start: Punch Fear in the Face, Escape Average and Do Work that Matters – Jon Acuff

https://amzn.to/2NPgYhm

www.ingramcontent.com/pod-product-compliance
Lightning Source LLC
Chambersburg PA
CBHW061835040426
42447CB00012B/2982